GIFTS FROM A GUIDE

LIFE HACKS FROM A SPIRITUAL TEACHER

DUKE TATE

DISCLAIMER

The information presented in this book is intended to be lifestyle tips for improving the quality and enjoyment of one's life and is not meant to diagnose, treat, or prescribe any medical conditions, nor does it exist to provide any licensed financial advice. If you are unwell, seek a medically trained doctor or psychiatrist to be treated properly; if you need sound financial advice, you should visit a financial advisor before acting.

CONTENTS

INTRODUCTION

From 2005 to 2012, I had the good fortune to study many areas of health and life under a Sufi guide and doctor named Ali Dede who was trained in various parts of the world. Dede is the director of Instituto Alef in Mexico. Many of the topics I learned along the way pertained to overcoming multiple chemical sensitivities, Lyme disease, hypoglycemia, and erectile dysfunction, which I write about in detail in the first book in the My Big Journey series, *Returning to Freedom: Breaking the Bonds of Chemical Sensitivities and Lyme Disease*. This book originally started out as a very small e-book I self-published titled *How to Live: The Guide to Looking Young, Feeling Great and Becoming Rich*, and since, after many many rewrites, transformed into this book you are now holding.

Dede trained under the famous Sufi master Idries Shah and his brother, Omar Ali Shah (Agha). On Instituto Alef's website, Dede outlines a very important concept that he calls "Health via the Five Elements." In it, he describes how health can be maintained through an adequate balance of the five elements: air, earth, water, fire, and spirit. If there is too much or too little of any one of these, or if one of these is polluted, illness can result. I go into specific aspects of these five elements in this book, but encourage all my readers to review his webpage thoroughly, as it is the wisest overview of health I have ever received. Also, Dede wrote a wonderful book about life for his children titled *Advice from a Sufi,* which is also for sale on his website: www.sufismo.com where it is available in English, Russian, and Spanish editions.

I hope everyone interested in my work will study Dede's teachings, as so much of what I learned came from this humble, wise, and remarkable man I was blessed to call my teacher for some time. I met him in 2005 after discovering his website through a Google search. I applied to become a student in his wonderful school and he accepted me and began attending to my health as well. While some of the knowledge in this book came from Dede, other observations (such as those on dating) come mostly from me. I suggest using this book like a manual that contains useful information about life and health. Surely, nothing happens or is written by chance, and this book is no exception.

Sufi Master Ali Dede

1

CHANGE YOUR THOUGHTS, CHANGE YOUR REALITY

The first step in learning how to live well is to understand that life is about choices. We can either make good choices or bad choices, but everything we do, we choose to do, consciously or unconsciously. When we make bad choices, we pay for it with consequences. Then, we spend a great deal of time complaining about the outcome of what started as a choice. Make good choices and spend time enjoying the outcome of those wonderful decisions.

The most important choice we can make is to control our thoughts. Thoughts have a power over what we manifest and attract into our lives, which people are now studying all over the world due to the hit movie *The Secret*. *The Secret* teaches the law of attraction, which states that "like attracts like." Thoughts have frequencies; like radio signals, thoughts send vibrations out into the universe that cause a corresponding signal to reverberate back to us. My Sufi guide Ali Dede described this as the mind being like an old-fashioned radio with a knob that can be tuned to a particular station such as "health," "fitness," "wealth," "happiness," etc. Unfortunately, many of us have a broken knob that is stuck on a bad channel like "money is bad" or "relationships suck," and so we keep thinking repetitive thoughts on that channel, thereby attracting those corresponding low frequencies. Repair your radio by turning the knob to a new positive channel, and set the frequencies for your life to occur.

Our radios are often stuck on these negative channels due to our upbringing. But a phenomenal tool exists to clear out unconscious intentions—Emotional Freedom Technique (EFT).

EFT is basically an emotional form of acupuncture that involves tapping one's fingers on the meridian points instead of using needles. EFT was developed by Gary Craig and is a combination of the radical forgiveness from *A Course in Miracles* written by Helen Schucman, Neuro-Linguistic Programming (NLP), and the meridian points outlined in Thought Field Therapy (a tapping technique developed by Roger Callahan, which he teaches and outlines in his book, *Tapping the Healer Within*). I suggest tapping as often as possible with a basic EFT recipe (which you can find online at EFT expert, Brad Yate's website: www. tapwithbrad.com) in order to clear out the negative thoughts that keep you stuck. Learn and remember this basic recipe because EFT will come up throughout this book. EFT Wizard Brad Yates has hundreds of videos on YouTube you can tap to and many great programs you can buy on his website. I used just one video from Brad Yates's YouTube channel titled "Sex Issues" for four consecutive days to cure my erectile dysfunction, which plagued me for years.

Now that you have this wonderful tool, let's explore four other very powerful tools that can help you to start living your best life today.

Let's now discuss your intention, which is also the second secret of *The Eleven Secrets of Spiritual Development* laid out by the Sufi master Khoja Abd Al-Khaliq al Ghujdwani of Turkestan. One of the first and foremost exercises Dede taught me was how to use my intention. We have already stated that life is about choices. If your mind is like a ship traveling through the ocean, your intentions are the steering wheel. Every morning, I state a list of my intentions for the day with positive affirmations. I usually do this during my morning inner work. Such an intention might be "I choose to have a wonderful day today" or "I choose to attract good health today."

"Gratitude is the key to success," Dede says. Take out a notepad or a journal, and write everything you are grateful for out like this, numbering one on: "I am so most especially grateful for..." If we recognize and affirm what we are grateful for, we will find that our life is already rich and full of blessings. Plus, this is a method for sending positive frequencies out to the universe, which (according to the law of attraction) will be answered with a corresponding frequency of "more to be grateful for."

After you finish your gratitude list, make a numbered *want* list. Start by writing down the first thing you want in your life and then keep writing every day, making the list longer and longer. Before things can manifest in your life, you must want them. Many teachers in the law of attraction community say that it is a person's "vibration" that attracts things to them, but it is really about what a person strongly desires. Otherwise, how can we explain why bad people can attract good things and even good people into their lives? Evidence of this abounds. Desire is the great manifester. Write "I want to have more financial success" or "I want to attract a wonderful mate into my life."

After you finish your intentions and your want and gratitude lists, it's time to perform a visualization. I recommend spending about ten minutes daily visualizing the positive life you want to live. See yourself living the life you dream about, and try to feel the emotions you will experience while doing it. Dede coined the following phrase about the importance of visualization: "Let us dedicate time to seeing things the way we want them to be, and what we want will become Reality."

Another manifestation tool you can use to these ends is a *vision board*. I usually print out images of things that inspire me, things I am grateful for, and things I want to attract into my life, and then affix these to a tack board. This could mean a new car you want to own, spiritual enlightenment, health, etc. The idea is that just by seeing these images every day and focusing on them with desire, it will assist you in attracting them into your life.

MEDITATION AND GUIDES

Meditation is a very important technique for staying centered and developing your spiritual life. I personally think that everyone should meditate for an average of fifteen to forty-five minutes a day. Studies have shown that meditation can increase wakeful, relaxed attention. Furthermore, if a person is searching for a spiritual teacher, there is no better place to start looking than within. Many *real teachers* in the outer world do not behave the way people want or expect them to; they often outwardly live very normal lives. Such teachers can be very hard to find. They do not advertise and recruit students like certain charlatan gurus. People have become fed up with even the idea of spiritual teachers thanks to con artists like Bikram Choudhury, who turned out to be a sexual predator posing as a guru. But the presence of such phony teachers does not preclude the existence of real teachers. There is a wise saying in the Sufi way: "The false coin exists only because there is a thing such as true gold." If you have had difficulty attracting a teacher in the outer world, then through meditation you may be able to contact a guide who has passed on. My journey started with a teacher in the world, but that doesn't have to be your story. Famous spiritual teachers like Gary Renard and Esther Hicks both were visited by guides while meditating; these guides became their teachers. The problem is most people don't sit in still silence for long enough to attract such a teacher. Most people in the West are hopelessly lost in the senseless act of *doing something else* all the time. Try *not doing something else* for a change, and be still. I was taught this exercise of *not doing something else* by my teachers over the course of years, and it has changed my life in many positive ways.

At the time of this writing, I have been meditating every day for almost fourteen years. Sometimes during this practice, I reflect and contemplate, which are also forms of meditation. Reflect on your life and see what comes up as you sit quietly in the stillness of the now without noise polluting your thoughts. Contemplate the spirituality of your life. Take notes on what comes to you. If you combine meditation with the reading spiritual books, you will have already engaged in a form of Inner Work. I have placed a list of books for this in the Recommended Reading and Resources section at the end of this book. While reading these books, it's highly possible that you will gain insight, be it from your guides or external reality. After I began reading spiritual books while suffering from Lyme disease, I started to have very spiritual and symbolic dreams. On one particularly poignant night, I dreamed I was in a jungle in South America, standing in front of a small stone altar covered in gold bullion. To my right stood a Sufi wearing an emerald green robe and hood. Later, when I met Dede, who had traveled all over South America and lived in Mexico, I understood the significance of the dream. He also taught me the investment value of precious metals, including gold. Reflect deeply on your dreams, and journal them. They may slowly reveal inner truths to you about life and yourself.

EMOTIONAL AND MENTAL HEALING

I f you have emotional distress, have tried the tools mentioned in the previous chapters, and still can't heal, you might try Bach Flower Remedies. Edward Bach (1886-1936) was an English homeopath who believed that the dew found on petals absorbed the properties of the plants. Through clinical trial and error, Bach discovered that the essences of different flowers were good remedies for different moods and emotions, and thus created Bach Flower Remedies.

If those don't work, it might be time for counseling or talk therapy, which can be very helpful for healing from all sorts of emotional trauma. If you have financial limitations, seek free counseling from Catholic charities or find a practitioner who is willing to work with you on a sliding scale. If Emotional Freedom Therapy is working for you, seek out an EFT practitioner like Brad Yates (the EFT Wizard). Your healing may be slow at first—especially if you have a lot of trauma—but in time, you will find that you will begin to heal.

Another useful technique to improve emotional well-being is to regulate your heart rate variability with *heart breathing*, developed by HeartMath. Heart rate variability monitors the time between heartbeats. When a person feels emotions such as joy, appreciation, and love, this variation is highly ordered and called a "coherent heart rhythm pattern." When a person feels fear, anger, and hate, the variation is highly erratic and called an "incoherent heart rhythm pattern." HeartMath's research has found that the activity of sensing your breath entering through the heart center while feeling gratitude can produce coherent heart rhythm patterns. Be sure to invest in the book *The Heart-Math Solution* and an EM wave device so you can monitor your heart breathing.

If you suffer from a mental illness such as bipolar disorder or an anxiety disorder (as I do), you may need to see a professional. I tested nearly every single natural remedy for mental health, including St. John's wort, Sam-E, lithium orotate and many others. While the lithium orotate did help some in improving my mood, nothing had a profound effect on my mental health until I got on the right medicine. You may need to consult with a psychiatrist, who can to prescribe you medicine for your disorder. Some mental disorders are nearly impossible to treat without medicine, and the people who live with them can become very unstable without the appropriate medicine—but with the right prescription, such people can live normal lives. That being said, I want you to know that for me to finally overcome my anxiety disorder took more than just the right medicine—it took faith.

BELIEVE IN MIRACLES

"The only thing we have to fear is fear itself."

— Franklin D. Roosevelt

I have always believed in miracles, but never truly knew they were possible until I overcame my anxiety disorder and embraced fearless living.

According to Our World Date, 264 million people suffer from anxiety. (Anxiety Association of America, n.d.) So, there is nothing to be ashamed of if you are one of them. In the grips of it, you may feel like it is the end of the world, but just remember the Sufi saying: "This too shall pass."

I suffered from crippling anxiety throughout most of my life. I was even an anxious kid. Looking back on it, I am not sure at what age it all started. Both of my parents were anxious types: perfectionists and obsessive compulsives, even though they had hearts of gold and were very loving. Since then, they too have embraced fearless living and are much happier because of it.

I became nervous early on about girls, starting in the

fourth grade. Whenever I had a crush on a girl, I would become frightened at the thought of talking to her. At some level I felt very self-conscious because I had more freckles than anyone I had ever known, and my freckles and red hair weren't always received with kindness by other children. I was even ridiculed on the playground for being redheaded. Ginger-phobia is a very real condition that affects many young children in America, and I was one of them. My anxiety started as a vague, generalized fear that always just hung there. At first, I was cautious of situations and had a tendency to overanalyze, reading into scenarios things that weren't actually there. I also began to crave foods and slowly developed an eating disorder, eating to calm my nerves. Dairy worked the best due to its high calcium content (which has a calming effect), but this unhealthy coping method caused me to gain weight.

I also drank caffeinated sodas with lots of sugar, like many other kids my age. Caffeine was a drug that proved its capacity for making me very unsettled, yet still I craved it. It made me feel alive and gave me the illusion of having more energy—although I would later come to understand that there is no real energy in caffeine, only artificial stimulation.

I also now know that I have a natural inclination toward anxiety due to my enneagram personality type. The enneagram personality system is an ancient personality typing system that states there are nine general types laid out along a circle, with point 9 at the top. Those nine types are: (9) The Peacemaker, (8) The Warrior, (7) The Adventurer, (6) The Loyalist, (5) The Observer, (4) The Creative, (3) The Winner, (2) The Helper, and (1) The Perfectionist. Each type has a single subtype: social, one-on-one, and survival. Each type also has a "wing" to another type on either side of it along the circle. For instance, a type 5 could have a type 4 or type 6 wing. These wings color the primary type by introducing behaviors from the other type. I began studying enneagrams at the age of seventeen at the insistence of my parents, and knowing about them has changed my view of the world dramatically. I am a type 8—The Warrior—which likes to be in charge and take command. It is one of the three extroverted types (7 and 3 being the other two).

My wing to type 7 on the chart (The Adventurer) explains my chronic anxiety, because type 7 is a very mentally active type. Witty, intellectual, and funny, their minds work very fast. They like to over-plan, travel, indulge in pleasures, eat, and have fun. This *monkey mind* characteristic of that type causes Adventurer individuals (even on the wings) to have overly active minds. Coffee and caffeine in general can be very problematic for members of these groups, and they almost ruined my life. They often cause these types to seem manic in some way, and many Adventurer types abstain from coffee.

My caffeine dependency was further complicated by my underage habit of smoking cigarettes. One day in 1994 at a friend's lake house in Rankin County, Mississippi, I began smoking cigarettes; I was thirteen. One of my good friends pulled out a pack of Camel Lights he had swiped from his sister and passed them around. I only took that first cigarette to be cool, but the moment I inhaled it, I was hooked. For the first time, I felt all the tension in my body release. The problem is that the effect wore off in thirty minutes, and I was craving another one like a rat in a cage. I didn't stop craving nicotine until recently, when I finally gave up cigars for good.

During late middle school and all throughout high school, I always had nicotine close at hand: dipping tobacco when I couldn't smoke, or wandering off into the woods to light up in private. I was drinking caffeinated sodas throughout the day as well. I was wiry and fun, but manic and scatter-brained. I wasn't really bipolar except during my freshman and sophomore years in high school, when I fell head over heels in love with a fellow classmate who didn't reciprocate my feelings. At that time, my mania oscillated with bouts of depression. Looking back on it all, it is not clear how many of my symptoms were seriously exacerbated by caffeine and nicotine dependence. Today, I take 5 mg of Lexapro for my anxiety disorder, which helps tremendously—but it also takes inner work to calm the condition. Medicine can only do part of the job.

Coffee addiction is a severe problem for many people. Over 70 percent of the world's population drinks coffee every day. Developed in Sufi monasteries in Yemen in the fifteenth century to enable longer periods of meditation, coffee is imbibed by nearly everyone these days. For many people, it's not a problem, but for people like myself, it is venom or troll juice ("troll juice" because it turns me into a troll when I drink it) causing its drinker to become unhinged, agitated, and jumpy. It is also one of the most acidic beverages in the world, which made it even worse for my personal health and well-being. In the hit sitcom *Frasier* that aired many years ago, the café in Seattle they frequented was called Café Nervosa. That pretty much sums up my thoughts about coffee. For me, coffee was a drug and I was a junkie. Even though I was an anxious type and caffeine exacerbated my symptoms, I was so addicted to it because I felt more in control when I was wired. I had also experienced a mild childhood learning disability that made me a slow reader, and caffeine accelerated my left brained "spotlight thinking". These days, as someone who reads over 100 pages on a good day with very little or no caffeine, I laugh about it all. Over time, I managed to train myself to read fast simply by repetition, but back then, I felt I needed a study aid.

Another problem that compounded my fight or flight attitude was that I had always breathed through my mouth. My father was a mouth-breather—perhaps I learned it from him. The problem with mouth-breathing is that it causes a mild level of hyperventilation because it is an emergency function that activates the "fight or flight" response in the body. The body thinks you are hunting, running, or in danger. It results in less oxygen transfer to the blood, whereas the nose produces nitric oxide, which allows for better absorption of oxygen in your lungs. Nitric oxide also allows your body to transport oxygen throughout the body and heart more effectively by dilating the blood vessels and relaxing vascular smooth muscle. (Caffaso, n.d.) Nothing has done more to lower my anxiety than becoming a nose-breather. It has a spiritually centering effect as well. I always imagined I could never retrain myself to nose-breath because my nose had been chronically congested since I was a small child. Yet after working with my Sufi guide, Ali Dede, I trained myself to nose-breath in a very short amount of time. So much of it is insistence and practice. Dede himself has a deviated septum and nose breathes.

Another very important exercise my guides taught me was to *not do something else*. Nervous, anxious types must learn to slow down. The more nervous they are, the more active they are: running around, cleaning, organizing, working, buying food, etc. I practiced the activity of not doing something else for over a year, on and off. This involved staying still in my room for long periods of time and not jumping up to run to the grocery store or walk the dog or any other mindless activity—just enjoying existence in the ever-expanding present. Anxiety is either about the past or the future, rarely the present—and the antidote to fear is faith. Nervousness is a lack of faith in God to protect you. As such, overcoming anxiety is a miracle that requires faith in the divine to back you up at every turn. Anxious types really suffer from a control issue—they believe only they can fix everything and stop impending disaster.

So—I believe in miracles, I have faith, I breathe through my nose, and I practice the Zen art of not doing something else.

5

INFLUENCES

As you walk the path of self-realization, you will find that external influences are some of the most important factors in your well-being and what you attract into your life. Be sure to always select the most positive influences you can. Reviewing positive things throughout the day over and over is very useful also.

When you're choosing a movie, try to focus on comedies or stories that make you feel good. There is a growing body of research that has shown laughter to be very beneficial for people on all levels. A feel-good movie might be a comedy like *What About Bob?* (1991) with Bill Murray or *The Holiday* (2006) with Kate Winslet. Something warm. I personally like the classics and watch a lot of old comedies. Movies like *It's a Wonderful Life* (1947) contain powerful messages about life and gratitude. When I was very ill, Dede advised that I surround myself with comedy DVDs. It's a known fact that Stephen Spielberg survived the filming of *Schindler's List* (1994) by watching *Seinfeld* episodes every night in his room.

Only listen to music that makes you feel good. Because music is emotional by nature, it can have a very strong effect on your personal emotional state. Negative music can really drag you down. Music by some very talented musicians whose work you may "like" can nonetheless have quite negative frequencies in it of hate, anger, fear, envy, greed, etc. For American music, I tend to listen to singer-songwriters. Standards also have good vibes, and I like Frank Sinatra, Steve Tyrell, and Tony Bennett. Van Morrison and Loreena McKennitt are my favorite spiritual musicians, and I think Italian singer Andrea Bocelli is a genius. Classical music has very high frequencies, and I am such a fan of Hans Zimmer.

Books are another influence which is very important to be conscious of, choosing them carefully. It has been said that all knowledge is recorded in books somehow, somewhere. If you are struggling with a problem in your life and want to improve it, turn to non-fiction books. With the self-help sections filled with books on how to change your life, there is no excuse for not taking the steps to start right away. Do your absolute best to try and be perceptive as to which teachers are false and which are legitimate.

I consider reading spiritual books, such as the teaching stories of the Sufi tradition, to be a spiritual practice. These stories were developed by enlightened masters and are layered with meaning that impacts the reader according to their level of understanding. In the Resources section at the end of this book, I link to the Idries Shah Foundation (ISF), which sells many of these—some of which can be read for free and are available in audio form on ISF's YouTube channel. The philosopher Idries Shah (1924-1996) wrote countless books full of amazing teaching stories. I recommend buying some and reading them again and again. His son, Tahir Shah, is now writing brilliant fiction with underlying spiritual messages as well. Invest in some of his wonderful books, such as *Scorpion Soup*, *Jinn Hunter*, and *Hannibal Fogg*, and take the journey today.

Many people have apprehensions about reading. We are living in a media-saturated culture of overstimulation, where books are not a part of everyone's lives. For people who have an aversion to reading, audiobooks are a great way to overcome this. In a way, these echo the early storytellers in the bazaars. Ali Dede once prescribed that I read a wonderful book titled *Bombshell* by former actress Suzanne Somers. One day he asked me how my reading of it was coming along, and I told him I found it very hard to read because there was a lot of nutritional science in it. I remember his simple astonished reply, "Oh my." After that, I changed my attitude about the book and decided to enjoy reading and learning from it, and from then on, I read it with ease. It was just my attitude about it that was stopping me. I thought it was hard, and therefore, *it was*. On another occasion, Dede had asked me to read a marketing book that I found terribly boring. After I finished, he asked me how it was. I told him it was a hideous book, really, and that I despised it. He followed with, "But did you learn one thing from it?" I replied that yes, I had surely learned one thing, and he in turn said, "If you learn only one thing from a book, then it was worth reading."

6

NUTRITION

I believe that the single most important factor in attracting what we want is to feel good physically, which can go a long way toward changing your outlook on life. The foods we eat can cause us to feel good or bad. It is so difficult to do inner work when our health is not serving us. My journey in the Great Tradition was really focused primarily on my health at first because I suffered from Lyme disease, multiple chemical sensitivities, erectile dysfunction, and chronic fatigue. I detail this journey in the first book in this series, *Returning to Freedom: Breaking the Bonds of Chemical Sensitivity and Lyme Disease*.

The most important nutritional aspect of health is to consume as many alkalinizing foods as possible. When the body is alkaline, one feels truly well; when it is acidic, a person feels unwell. Some foods have an alkalinizing effect on the body whereas others acidify. Please thoroughly familiarize yourself with an alkaline and acidic food chart (available online). An alkaline body is truly a healthy body.

The most alkalinizing foods on the planet are raw organic vegetables and fruits, their juices, and apple cider vinegar. Choosing organic foods generally means choosing foods that were grown without pesticides. Raw fruits and vegetables are also healthier because the enzymes, vitamins, and minerals in them are unadulterated. These live nutrients feed, heal, detoxify, and alkalinize the body. Dede says an alkaline body gives the correct internal hygiene to prevent disease. To track your levels of acidity, obtain pH test strips and measure your urine throughout the day. Levels of urine measure 0.8 lower on the pH scale than the reading on the pH paper, so you need to add 0.8 to the measurement. A urine pH measurement of 7.2-7.4 is ideal for cellular health to be present.

If you are having trouble maintaining an alkaline urine level, making a tonic of 1 teaspoon of sodium bicarbonate (baking soda), a full glass of unpolluted water, and some unheated honey can really help. Please note that experts discourage drinking this concoction more than once a day.

I love model and raw food activist Carol Alt's raw food books. She became an expert on raw foods after curing herself of cancer with them (under a doctor's guidance) and is truly knowledgeable on the subject. I try to always have a raw fruit and vegetable juice for breakfast. This is predominately a green juice made of celery, apple, grapes, and carrot. Beets are very good to juice as well. Although kale is very popular, its juice, along with other ingredients like ginger (in large amounts) and cilantro, can be particularly strong, and it might be better to use predominately milder ingredients at first or use those in smaller amounts. If you don't already have one, invest in a good centrifugal juicer like those from Champion or Green Star that won't oxidize the juices.

Be mindful of how you feel after starting your juice routine. Raw foods can cause detoxification, but most people just feel better. If you experience the negative effects of any detoxification, slow down.

When choosing what foods to eat, practice *conscious intuitive eating*, which means searching out those healthy foods that you crave. You can do this with cooked foods as well. The idea behind this is that your body intuitively knows what it needs in terms of the nutritional content of the foods you eat. And eat half your appetite always! Overeating alone can make a person feel very unwell, and restaurants in the US especially tend to serve ridiculously large portions.

The best fats to eat and cook with in ample amounts are organic grass-fed butter, coconut oil, and olive oil with more moderation. Butter and coconut oil, as Dede says, have been vilified by economic interests, but have been part of a healthy diet for people all over the world for centuries. The outrage over coconut oil comes from the fact that it is a saturated fat. However, the saturated fat in coconut oil is a medium-chain fatty acid, not a long-chain fatty acid like those found in meat. The consumption of these medium-chain saturated fats actually causes less heart disease. We can look at the countries who consume coconut oil daily to demonstrate this, such as the Pacific Islands, which have the lowest rates of heart disease in the world among the people who adhere to their traditional diets and do not turn to processed Western foods. The Pukapuka and Tokelau Island study is one of the most thorough research studies conducted on a population with a high-fat diet coming primarily from coconuts. In the study, when compared to Western standards, the overall health of both groups was extremely good. The populations had ideal weight-to-height ratios when using the body mass index figures popular with nutritionists. Atherosclerosis and heart disease were rare conditions for both groups, and the Tokelauns derived 60 percent of their energy from fat—almost all of that being saturated fat derived from coconuts. (Fife, 2013)

Coconut oil can go a long way toward stabilizing blood sugar, too. I took coconut oil multiple times every day to cure my hypoglycemia, and my father who suffered with medically diagnosed hypoglycemia has as well. You can read more about my epic health journey in my book *Returning to Freedom: Breaking the Bonds of Chemical Sensitivity and Lyme Disease*. Coconut oil has been shown to have a remarkable effect on the pancreas.

Butter from grass-fed cow milk is a wonderful superfood that is rich in omega-3 fatty acids. Omega-3's are essential fatty acids (EFAs—polyunsaturated fats) that the body can't synthesize on its own but are necessary for normal metabolism. Therefore, they must come from food. There are three main types of omega-3 fats: a-linolenic acid (ALA), eicosapentaenoic acid (EPA), and docosahexaenoic acid (DHA). Foods rich in omega-3s include wild, oily fishes like cod, salmon, mackerel, krill, anchovies, bluefish, herring, lake trout, sardines, sturgeon, and tuna, as well as algae like E3, chlorella, grass-fed butter, nuts like walnuts, grains such as flaxseed and its oil, and oils like canola and soybean. (Axe D. , 2019)

Many doctors and nutritionists now believe that an imbalance of omega-3s with omega-6s (found in corn) and 9s (olive oil) are responsible for inflammation and some heart disease.

Superfoods

Regarding what foods to eat (cooked or raw), there is a wonderful book written by Dr. Stephen Pratt, MD, called *Superfoods Rx*. The book lists fourteen superfoods that are the most nutrient-dense foods we can consume (he now lists twenty-four foods on his website). His book is truly fascinating because he gets right down into the phytonutrients, vitamins, and minerals that are found in foods. You will learn about things like how the flavonoids in the orange skins found in marmalade are good for you, and how wild-caught salmon is rich in omega-3s. I strongly recommend reading his book and incorporating his fourteen primary superfoods into your diet: beans, blueberries, broccoli, turkey, yogurt, salmon, walnuts, oats, soy, oranges, pumpkin, spinach, tomatoes, and tea.

In addition to Dr. Pratt's foods, I also consider white rice, wine, yams, kefir, flaxseed, and blackstrap molasses (very rich in iron and potassium) to be superfoods. (Steven G. Pratt, 2006)

Super Spices

Let's not forgot super spices. Countries like Mexico, Thailand, Morocco, and India use spices such as chili, turmeric, and cayenne in ample amounts in their cooking; this has many truly outstanding effects on the body.

I love spicy food, especially Mexican, in no small part thanks to the chili pepper. The same goes for Thai food. Chili peppers contain capsaicin, which many believe reduces inflammation due to its inhibition of substance P (a neuropeptide). It also increases circulation, which in turn alleviates many ails. A little cayenne may help improve cardiovascular health and sinuses, relieve pain, and boost immunity. It's also rich in vitamin A and beta-carotene, hence its bold red color. (Ruggeri, 2019) Incorporate it into your cooking to add a Mexican flavor, or talk to your health pro about taking a cayenne supplement. Sometimes, if I have a sore throat, just putting some cayenne in a glass of water can sometimes do away with it.

Turmeric is another super spice, long championed in the East for its flavor. The real benefits of turmeric come from its antioxidant curcumin, which gives the spice its yellow color. Curcumin has been shown to reduce inflammation, provide antioxidants, and benefit brain, cardiac, and metabolic health. Unfortunately, the curcumin in turmeric isn't absorbed very well by the GI tract, so taking the extract is a better way to go. My uncle, David Tate, normalized his cholesterol and rid himself of arthritis with curcumin. I have taken it with very good results but advise you start very slowly if you choose to take it. You would be wise to speak to your health pro before starting any new supplement routine.

Fountain of Youth

We all are searching for the fountain of youth—some eternal elixir that will help us live a long time. I used to live in St. Augustine, the oldest city in America, founded by Ponce de Leon in his search for the elusive fountain of youth.

That was a legend, but there is a real place where people drink from such a fountain, in the Caucasus Mountains in the former Soviet Union's southernmost point. The people of this region are the some of the healthiest people in the world, boasting some of the highest numbers of centenarians. This area is cold and rugged, replete with snow and treacherous passes. So what fountain are the Caucus people drinking from? It's simple really: kefir. Kefir—a beverage of fermented cow's milk—originated in this region and was considered a gift from God by the tribal peoples, given to them by the Prophet Mohammed. People would take it on long journeys through the mountains in order to sustain them. The word literally means "to feel good." And why is that? Kefir contains naturally occurring beneficial bacteria (probiotics) that strengthen our bodies and our digestive tracts. Kefir has an effervescent quality like ginger ale and goes well with fruit and honey. Other forms of good bacteria are found in Greek yogurt and oral probiotic supplements.

Red Wine

In moderation, red wine is another superfood. It contains resveratrol, polyphenols (antioxidants found in the grape skins), and rare trace minerals. Not to mention, it tastes good! Plus, wine makes for a wonderful intellectual and social hobby—every varietal and year tastes unique based on the grapes, process, region where it was grown, and the weather that growing season. I think it's a blast exploring these different aspects of *vino* with friends and family.

However, the antioxidant resveratrol may be the real secret to red wine's benefits. There's a lot of research coming out based on studies in mice that suggests a little daily resveratrol may protect the heart. And it's known that moderate amounts of alcohol can help raise a person's good cholesterol. That's not to say you should guzzle a bottle a day—following the American dictum that if a little is good, a lot must be great (please, everything in moderation)—but it may explain the French paradox of that country's seemingly healthier hearts than the Americans' in spite of a diet rich in cholesterol-dense foods.

So why is red wine good and not white wine? Well, the secret is in the dark skins, which are often suggested to contain more antioxidants. It is also rich in minerals as well.

If you can't drink alcohol, you might speak to your health pro about taking a daily resveratrol supplement. Keep in mind, some of the resveratrol supplement brands offer dosages that may be too high for you. Dede suggested the best dosage for most people to be around 25 mg a day.

If you've never had red wine and you're interested in getting started, I'll give you a brief rundown. There are three primary red grapes (as far as the American bartender is concerned): Merlot, Cabernet Sauvignon, and Pinot Noir. Every grape and vineyard's wine tastes different based on its soil, geography and climate. Find one you like. Keep in mind that expensive isn't always better—there are some very good moderately priced wines on the market. If you get headaches, try buying a sulfite-free wine.

Optimal Diet

By now, you may be overwhelmed by asking yourself which diet is "the best." There are hundreds of diets out there, and choosing between them can be quite baffling. The diet that Ali Dede recommended for me is the one described in *The Zone* by Dr. Barry Sears, which dictates a balance of protein, carbs, and fats to keep your eicosanoid hormone levels up. Doctor Sears has said that The Zone isn't a diet at all but a way of eating to get the correct hormonal response from your food every time you eat. One can't really consume vegetable juices in the zone, so don't worry about eating every meal this way—just try to eat some of your meals in the recommended proportions. Also, review *The China Study* by Dr. T. Colin Campbell, which details the largest nutritional study ever conducted on a population. Campbell found that when the Chinese people ate a diet rich in fruits, vegetables and grains and sparse in dairy and meat there were far fewer incidences of cancer and heart disease. I am not advocating a strict vegetarian diet, but considering *The China Study*, it is advisable to eat less meat and dairy than is typically found in a Western diet. That being said, I am by no means a vegetarian—deliciously prepared meat dishes are some of my favorite things to eat. They also are acidifying, however, and since an alkaline body is a healthy body, always be mindful of your alkalinity when consuming meat. While the paleo and Atkins diets are all the rage for losing weight and staying fit these days, Dr. Atkins himself died obese, weighing 258 pounds, with hypertension and a history of heart attacks and congestive heart failure.

Hydration

Staying hydrated is truly another key to good health. Drinking the cleanest spring water available in your area is best. Placing it in a Vitalizer Plus machine, which uses a magnet at the bottom of the pitcher will lend it a hexagonal or crystalline molecular structure. Water loses its structure due to pollutants and traveling in straight lines through pipes. High glacial lakes and certain springs have this crystalline structure. (Flanagan, 2016) Also, you can place a hydrogen capsule like PrimoH2 in a pitcher of hexagonal water to give the water more molecular hydrogen. Almost all water today is deficient in hydrogen—the most powerful antioxidant in the world. Spring and alkaline water are essentially dead. Living water is hexagonal and hydrogen-rich.

Caffeine and Smoking

So many people drink coffee daily, and most want to know if it is healthy or not. Lines of vehicles wrap around Starbucks stores all over America at every hour of the day. Coffee is big business throughout the world. However, it also happens to be one of the most acidic beverages you can consume, so you might opt for cold brew, which is far less acidic since the hot water causes oils to release which are full of acidic compounds. Always be mindful of your alkalinity level when drining it. If you have an overactive mind, you may want to cut caffeine altogether or drink green tea instead, which contains about 30 percent polyphenols by weight and is alkalinizing. Coffee has always been venom for me because I naturally have a very active mind, and too much can make me very anxious. Drinking too much coffee caused me to hyperactively move when I was younger and almost ruined my life. When I'm driving my 38′ RV for over seven hours in one day, I do drink green tea. At such times, the caffeine is very useful for concentration. I used to think I had to have it to read and write, but these days I find I am much more focused and centered in those tasks without it.

It is best to do away with smoking of any frequency, especially in our modern world where so many pollutants are already working against us in many cases. Your health will thank you for it.

7

OPTIMAL NUTRIENTS

My grandfather on the Tate side, Irwin, was passionate about nutrition. A bodybuilder in his spare time, he started taking supplements in the 1960s before anyone knew what they were. He used to read *Life Extension* magazine and was always aware of the latest cutting-edge research on nutrition and health. When I went to his place in Palm Beach, Florida, in 2000, the top three kitchen cabinets were full of supplement bottles—probably around fifty of them. My grandfather was in incredible health for his age, but sometimes he took too many nutrients because he thought if one was good, twelve would be better.

Take nutritional supplements seriously. They are powerful. I recommend starting very slowly with any new nutrients. It takes time for the body to adjust to new vitamins and minerals, foods and medicines. If you start slowly and gradually work up (if you need to), always being in tune with how your body is responding, then your body will thank you for it. If you start out with a full dosage, it may shock your system and make you feel ill. Furthermore, too many supplements can cause acidity. If you've never taken nutrients, speak to your health professional or someone skilled in applied kinesiology about adding one in at a time. Prioritize the desired effects based on your conditions. This doesn't mean you can't take six nutrients—just be conscious of what you're taking, what they're for, and how your body reacts. Always proceed very carefully and never force anything. People's bodies are different; just because someone else does well on a particular supplement doesn't mean it is necessarily right for you.

The first three supplements I want to introduce for daily usage aren't supplements at all, but superfoods.

Sun Chlorella

Sun Chlorella is a nutrient-dense superfood and a potent detoxifier of toxins and heavy metals as well, making it truly unique. It is known to be a very good source of vitamin A (beta-carotene), chlorophyll, omega-3 and omega-6 and minerals, to name a few.

Probiotics

I take a daily probiotic, which we discussed in the section about kefir. Basically, there can be good and bad bacteria in the digestive tract. The good bacteria are very healthy because they help break down our food. There are literally billions of these microscopic helpers in our stomachs. However, due to overprescribed antibiotics and chlorine in our drinking water, probiotics have to be replenished every day. Bad bacteria should be avoided at all costs.

Marine Phytoplankton

My third daily superfood supplement is marine phytoplankton. The brand I feel is the best is Ocean's Alive. Each drop of this nutrient contains 5 billion identical cells of energy. Packed with phyto-nano nutrients consisting of *Nannochloropsis gaditana*, *Nannochloropsis galasemis*, and concentrated purified sea mineral trace elements, this food is truly unique.

Magnesium

The most important nutrient in my opinion that isn't found in food in significant quantities is magnesium. Magnesium deficiency can cause muscle aches or spasms, anxiety, hypertension, cardiovascular disease, poor digestion, and trouble sleeping. This important mineral is involved in over 300 biochemical functions in the body, such as regulating heartbeat rhythms and helping neurotransmitter functions. Magnesium is known as the "calming mineral," and people often notice they feel more relaxed after consuming it. Unless you are eating lots of spinach, Swiss chard, pumpkin seeds, and beans, you're likely not getting this important mineral. (Levy J. , Magnesium Benefits, Dosage, Recommendation and Best Types, 2019) Like vitamin C, it is depleted every day and must be replenished. Today, the soils that grow our produce are very deficient in minerals like magnesium, so supplementation corrects this.

CoQ10

Another important nutrient that isn't readily available in our food is coenzyme 10, or CoQ10. Produced by the body and used for everyday functions including cellular energy, it is a fat-soluble antioxidant that transports electrons around the body and protects against damaging oxidative stress. Some of its benefits include boosted stamina, sustained energy levels, defense against free radicals (highly reactive molecules with an "odd" electron on the external orbit, creating an imbalance that turns these fragmented molecules into unstable biochemical agents), a reduction in the signs of aging, and support for a healthy cardiovascular system. (Levy J. , What Is CoQ10? 8 Benefits for Energy, Aging, and Brain and Heart Health, 2019)

Anyone who takes cholesterol medicine should speak to their qualified health professional about adding CoQ10, because cholesterol medicine stops the production of CoQ10 in the body.

Vitamin C

Vitamin C is a water-soluble vitamin that acts as a powerful antioxidant. Found in certain fruits and vegetables such as oranges, acerola cherries, bell peppers, papayas, grapefruits, and kiwis—to name a few—many claim it boosts immunity and helps fight free radicals, which can cause damage to cells. In the 1700s, scurvy was a leading cause of death among British sailors and was cured by an intake of lemon juice (the cause was ultimately determined to be a vitamin C deficiency). Vitamin C is also a common ingredient in skin care products because it's involved in the synthesis of collagen. When suffering with an autoimmune disorder or the common cold, you might look into supplementing with 1,000 mg daily to boost immunity. (Link, Vitamin C Benefits the Immune System - and So Much More, 2019)

Vitamin A

Vitamin A is a fat-soluble vitamin linked to healthy vision and proper functioning of the immune system and organs. Many experts now believe it may be even more important to the body's immune function than vitamin C. The best food source is cod liver oil—just one teaspoon contains 90 percent of the recommended daily intake! Not to mention, it's a great source of vitamin D and omega-3s as well.

Vitamin B17

The Hunza tribe of Northern Pakistan eats fifty cooked bitter apricot seeds a day, which contain high levels of vitamin B17, and this tribe never gets cancer. Many people believe cancer is a vitamin B17 deficiency and that studies on the medical drug form of vitamin B17, *Laetrile*, in the 1970's were deliberately falsified at Sloan Kettering Cancer Center in New York, according to advocate Ralph Moss, the Assistant Director of Public Affairs at the time. (Griffin, 1974)

Iodine

Iodine is another vital nutrient many people are deficient in due to low levels in our food. Unless you live in Japan and eat kelp or dulse every day, you probably don't receive important amounts of this nutrient. Iodine is necessary for the thyroid gland to function properly. It is especially important in today's world where we consume lots of chlorinated drinking water. Chlorine, a halogenic trace mineral, also stores in the thyroid in place of iodine because they are both halogens (the body doesn't distinguish between them). If you swim a lot, it's especially important for you to take this nutrient (Cousens, n.d.). I like the supplement Iodoral by Optimox, which I take every day.

Resveratrol

One nutrient that I consider to be very interesting and exciting is resveratrol, which we already discussed briefly as being a polyphenol found in red wine. It has been shown in laboratory studies to promote longevity in cell cultures and animals. It reduces oxidative stress and even helps with cancer suppression. (Axe D. J., 2017) The correct dosage is on the lower end, around 25 mg a day.

Oxygen

If you've struggled with some ailment that you haven't been able to get relief from, you might speak to your health professional about a daily oxygen supplement like Cellfood. You can read all about my journey with oxygen in my book *Returning to Freedom: Breaking the Bonds of Chemical Sensitivity and Lyme Disease*. Oxygen is the single most vital element for our health and energy. I took Cellfood, breathed from a machine called the Aranizer, which electrically produces oxygen molecules O_4 through O_{10} (now going by the name of Pure Air for Life) and drank aranized water to cure myself of candidiasis and multiple chemical sensitivities. Another benefit of oxygen supplementation is that oxygen is aerobic and many bacteria and yeast are anaerobic, which means they can't survive in a highly oxygenated environment. A little oxygen boost every day might help keep your immune system strong.

Cellfood was developed by Everett Storey, a scientist involved in the development of the triggering mechanism that enabled the hydrogen bomb and a man whom Albert Einstein called "a genius." Storey and his colleagues all experienced radiation poisoning after years of working on the Manhattan Project. The Manhattan Project created the first nuclear weapons during War World II through research and development.

Storey decided he was going to use his genius to cure himself and so created Cellfood—a dissolved oxygen supplement containing 34 enzymes, 17 amino acids, and 78 minerals for a total of 129 nutrients. After taking this substance regularly, he cured himself and returned to living a healthy life. (Everett Storey: Turning the Harmful into Something that Saves Lives, 2016)

I took Cellfood everyday par Ali Dede's instruction as part of my therapy to get over chronic candidiasis, Lyme Disease and chemical sensitivities.

Natural Bug Killer

Colloidal silver is nanoparticles of silver suspended in water made through a process of electrolysis. It is widely available at most health food stores throughout America for consumption. Even the World Health Organization (WHO) uses silver and colloidal silver in water filtration in developing countries as researchers have found silver to be harmful to many bad bacteria, while being one of the least harmful metals to humans at the nanoparticle size.

Metal Toxicity

Not too long ago, I had my amalgam fillings removed by a dentist in Wellington, Florida who specializes in cosmetic dentistry and amalgam removal. Not only are amalgam fillings unattractive, but with the convenience and ease of composite fillings, they simply aren't practical anymore. After having them removed, I took a mixture of cilantro and chlorella in an extracted form sold as Metal Magic by Baseline Nutritionals (founded by nutrition expert Jon Barron). A Metal Magic clinical study was done at the Optimal Wellness Test Research Center in Nevada and the results of the 42-day test showed an 87 percent chelation of lead, 91 percent for mercury, and 74 percent chelation of aluminum. (Clinical Study Reveals First, Natural Formula Effective For Removing Heavy Metals, 2005) Many believe aluminum can cause unusual effects in the body, and aluminum cookware should be done away with as well. If you suspect you may have a metal toxicity issue, you can have a hair analysis test done to determine your levels.

8

QUANTUM PULSE

W hen I was very ill, one machine—the Vibe Machine—helped me tremendously. My family owned two of these devices, one for myself and the other for my parents. Developed by Gene Koonce, a Colorado electronic repair store owner and former army missile technician who worked on inventions in his spare time, the Vibe Machine (now going by the name Quantum Pulse) is a triumphant breakthrough in the field of energy medicine. The machine uses spectrum tubes that contain noble gases (that fall between the infrared and ultraviolet spectrum range) and a multi-wave oscillator, the combination producing biophotonic light in an electromagnetic field within a radius of six to eight feet around the machine. (The Device and the Inventor, n.d.)

The first time Dede recommended I try the Vibe Machine, I was in Half Moon Bay, California, just south of San Francisco with my mother, Charme Tate, visiting a chiropractor's house right on the ocean. Half Moon Bay is a truly picturesque town that crests along the Pacific. Home to one of the largest and most brutal waves, Maverick, that surfers love to ride, it's a hip town with a truly California vibe where people still ride horses on the beach. This humble middle-aged lady who owned the vibe machine, Dr. Joe, from Clarksdale, Mississippi had the clearest light blue eyes I had ever seen (other than those of the raw food guru, Aajonus Vonderplanitz), she surfed every day, and had a radiant glow to her skin. She informed us she used the machine for ten minutes a day everyday. We sat close to it in a dark room for three minutes while the machine made a loud noise and the glass tubes lit up as the various gases flowed through them. The physical effect was immediate: the sensation of increased energy in the body, peace, and calm.

9

EXERCISE

E xperts agree that it is essential to get a minimum of fifteen minutes of cardiovascular exercise every day. Strength training on machines or with free weights is also very good for the body. Many people are into CrossFit now, a high intensity form of weight training and cardio. I think that is truly wonderful. If you don't like working out with weights, you can pick up an activity like swimming instead. However, you get your exercise, as long as you address your fitness goals from a place of mental well-being, having a muscular physique looks and feels better.

Qi-Gong

Energy movements like the Chinese qi-gong are very beneficial also. Qi-gong is especially popular in California due to its proximity to Asia. I remember when I lived in Santa Monica in Los Angeles, groups of people would perform qi-gong in the California sun along Palisades Park in the mornings.

The Chinese believe that *qi*, or life force, circulates throughout the whole body and can become blocked at certain points due to many factors; such blockages can then cause illness. Performing certain movements as in qi-gong, or so the tradition insists, keeps the energy flowing properly. My favorite form of qi-gong is the one Ali Dede prescribed that I study—Spring Forest qi-gong. The creator of Spring Forest, Master Lin, trained with qi-gong masters for years in China. The Mayo Clinic has found in studies that Spring Forest can alleviate chronic pain. I also recommend performing pa tuan chin everyday. You can learn and perform the *pa tuan chin* qi-gong movement for health on my YouTube channel:

https://www.youtube.com/
channel/UCPsBoqTpCgHeyYx7fijEYOw

Other Forms of Exercise

If you're interested in strengthening your core, you might try paddle boarding—a truly fun and strengthening exercise. I like exercises that are fun and engaging, like skiing or surfing. These sports can be dangerous and difficult, however, so only practice them with a trained professional at first, and never go out alone. I kayak fish for fun, which has been an amazing workout for me.

I also think martial arts, especially aikido (translated from Japanese as "the way of harmonious spirit") are very useful for developing oneself physically while simultaneously strengthening the mind and spirit. Dede is a master at aikido, which emphasizes self-defense by using an opponent's energy against them without inflicting injury. Aikidio was developed by Japanese *Osensei* ("Great Teacher") Morihea Ueshiba (1883-1969) to unify his martial arts practice, religious beliefs, and philosophy. Ueshiba wrote a wonderful book titled *The Art of Peace* that I have included in the recommended reading. It can be purchased on Instituto Alef's website, found in the Resources section of this book.

Super Protein

If you're a weightlifter who is having trouble making gains, instead of wearing yourself out at the gym, you might investigate the "super protein" of raw, grass-fed milk. I used raw grass-fed milk for years when lifting to increase gains and maximize my flat bench press to 245 pounds—a huge change from the skinny freshman I was at Ole Miss in 2004 who could barely lift 145. My good friend, the raw food guru Aajonus Vonderplanitz (1947-2013), told me he used to go to the Venice Beach Gold's Gym when Arnold Schwarzenegger would work out there in his competition days, and everyone knew Schwarzenegger drank raw milk because it was superior for building muscle mass. The former California governor has even stated that he grew up eating raw egg shakes while lifting weights when he was younger because he didn't always have much money for food. In the back of his *Encyclopedia of Bodybuilding*, the former governor also recommends a raw egg and peanut butter shake for big gains. Raw eggs, like raw milk, build muscle very quickly. I won't argue the benefits or dangers of eating raw eggs, but will let you do your own research on this. I will say that if you have ever had a Caesar salad, you have probably eaten raw egg. When I was in Japan, I could order sashimi eggs at most restaurants, when they place a raw egg on your plate and you crack the egg over your bowl at your table. Japan has one of the lowest rates of cancer in the world, whereas the US has one of the highest rates of cancer—at least as of 2018 according to the American Institute for Cancer Research (ranking fifth in the world). Just know, for decades, bodybuilders and athletes have eaten raw eggs daily for muscle gain and maintenance.

"Cleanliness is next to Godliness," as the saying goes. In my opinion, hygiene and cleanliness of farms, kitchens and food preparation is one the biggest factors in disease transmission. The Japanese due to their emphasis on hygiene maintain some of the cleanest kitchens in the world. People should protect themselves by ensuring hygiene is maintained by their food sources starting from the farm to the table.

On November 21, 1976, the movie *Rocky* was released, and the whole world got to watch Sylvester Stallone break a bunch of eggs into a glass and drink them straight. On the WWE wrestler Hulk Hogan's TV show *Hogan Knows Best*, he also would occasionally eat a raw egg on camera. And more recently, the Rock's character in the movie *Hobbs and Shaw* eats raw eggs and chews coffee grinds for breakfast.

A lot of controversy surrounds raw milk, but I believe it is perfectly safe and healthy if it comes from an organic grass-fed source and is consumed shortly after production. Now it is also legal in twelve states. Widespread pasteurization laws in the 1930s centered around raw milk that came from so-called "swill milk" dairy farms that kept their cows in horrible conditions and fed them the mash byproduct from making hard liquor. These cows were very unhealthy —even the pasteurized milk they produced was bluish in color. (Schmid, 2009)

Studies occurring as early as 1938 by the drug and cosmetic industries found that raw milk did not support the growth of many pathogens, whereas heating milk promoted the growth of harmful bacteria by inactivating inhibins. Raw milk is often blamed as the culprit behind *Listeria monocytogenes*; however, a 2003 FDA/USDA report found that pasteurized milk had 29 times more instances of L-mono than raw milk. (Intrepretive Summary – Listeria Monocytogenes Risk Assessment, 2003) Deli meat has been proven to cause more foodborne illness, but the FDA doesn't claim that deli meat is unsafe—yet it does claim that "raw milk is inherently dangerous and should not be consumed." Why? It's something to reflect deeply on. There is an inherent prejudice against a simple food product people have been safely consuming since the beginning of time, and I suspect financial interests are at play. For one, pasteurization prolongs shelf life, which is an advantage for the companies selling it.

10

PERSONAL PRODUCTS

Whether you are health conscious or not, one important step in learning how to live is to clean up your body products. I personally get my shampoo, conditioner, and toothpaste from the Whole Foods chain of grocery stores. I look for natural shampoos with jojoba oil in them and for fluoride-free toothpastes like Jason Power Smile. Not to brag, but I personally have very white teeth and I believe the organic toothpastes are superior whiteners. There are also many handmade soaps that are superior alternatives to washing your body with harmful chemicals.

Aromatherapy

When selecting perfumes and colognes, it's important to understand aromatherapy—the ancient art of extracting the essences of plants and flowers in order to lift the spirit and alleviate some ailments.

The cologne and perfume industry have this theory at its foundation, even if the knowledge has been lost in favor of pleasing smells. Regardless, certain aromas do make us feel well. Perhaps the scent brings back a wonderful memory associated with it. Maybe a loved one wore a certain perfume and smelling it triggers their memory, or the fragrance has some other sort of special effect on you. Find that fragrance and wear it.

Perfumes and colognes are a great way to experience a daily emotional uplift. Experiment with the use of different fragrances to feel different ways. Many people do not tolerate mainstream colognes and perfumes well because of the toxic elements in them; such individuals often do well with essential oils. After experimenting with some different aromas, you may notice that you're drawn to certain ones when experiencing an emotion. For instance, if you're nervous, lavender may relax you; if you are depressed, rose oil may bring you joy.

Many modern air fresheners are full of toxic chemicals like formaldehyde—avoid these and artificially scented candles. I diffuse only the best essential oils in my place using an electronic diffuser. Dede prescribed that I use Bulgarian rose oil from a reputable online dealer. I get my frankincense, myrrh, lavender, and sandalwood from Scents of the Earth and my chamomile and eucalyptus from Aura Cacia.

Regarding women's makeup, Whole Foods offers a lot of good alternatives to regular makeup which can contain toxic chemicals. Fortunately, it seems like the industry is finally catching up with many brands in terms of using more healthy natural ingredients than they used to.

11

HEALTHY DWELLING

Getting rid of harsh chemical cleaners in favor of natural alternatives can go a long way to reducing your exposure to toxic chemicals, which are unnatural to the body. I buy my laundry and dish-washing detergents from a company called Seventh Generation. I clean my kitchen with an ecological degreaser called Bio-Kleen, which I dilute and use on my surfaces as well as the floors. Seventh Generation makes a degreaser also. I still use bleach for toilets and to clean my white laundry (but not every time). The silver nanotechnology company Pure Green 24's cleaning products, which formerly went by the name IV-7, is recommended by the EPA for destroying pathogens on contact.

Unless you live in the French Alps or have well water, you might strongly consider filtering the water that enters your home. It will make baths feel like a hot spring. Some municipalities add chlorine to the water supply, which they don't filter out afterward. Furthermore, many obscure chemicals and even drug residues get into tap water because the facilities where they're produced don't filter their wastewater.

A good filtration system will remove most of these harsh chemicals. In America, there are a lot of these systems on the market. Culligan and Pelican are two big names—their systems are very nice, and most areas have technicians for the installation as well as filter changes. Look for a carbon filter on the system you buy.

If you have a swimming pool or hot tub, I suggest making the migration to a salt-water chlorine generator. We all love to swim, but you know that feeling of getting out of a chlorinated pool—your hair is a little brittle and lighter and you smell like a chemical plant. With a water chlorine generator, salt water passes over the chlorine generator cells and produces hypochlorous acid, which is the same thing chemical chlorine makes when it's added to water. Then, a mild amount of saltwater is added to the water (much less than the ocean) to give your skin that smooth feeling.

If you want to clean the air in your house, you might also consider some air washers. I used to have terrible sensitivities to chemicals many years ago, which I detail in my book *Returning to Freedom: Breaking the Bonds of Chemical Sensitivities and Lyme Disease*. Back then, three machines saved my life. The first was the standalone IQ Air Health Pro Plus. It did the job where other HEPA air filters had failed. What makes the Swedish-made IQ Air unique is its Hyper HEPA filtration, which filters particles a hundred times smaller than regular HEPA filtration and ten times smaller than the average virus. Plus, it allows for installing an odor and smoke filter that will trap even the worst gases. The second machine was a truly exceptional polyatomic oxygen generator called the Aranizer, now going by the name Pure Air for Life. It electronically produces a whole range of oxygen molecules from O_4 to O_{10}, which bind with toxins in the room in your home. The third machine is a negative ion generator called the Elanra. As you may know, indoor and outdoor air pollution creates positive ions, which may adversely affect our health. Negative ions, on the other hand, found abundantly near oceans, trees, and mountains, are beneficial to human health, but the wind blows these negative ions away. You hear about this with the Santa Ana winds in Los Angeles which pollute the air with positive ions. Placing an Elanra in your home may ensure that you have optimal indoor air quality. They also have a portable unit that I like and often take with me in my car.

If you are interested in improving your indoor air quality (IAQ) aside from my list of the top air washers, you might also invest in some houseplants. NASA conducted a clean air study that tested which plants were the best at absorbing indoor air pollutants such as volatile organic compounds (VOCs), benzene, formaldehyde, and trichloroethylene (all of which are found in paints, adhesives, and carpets). Most of the plants on the list had evolved in subtropical and tropical environments and were able to photosynthesize light well. The following plants were some found to be the top air scrubbers: bamboo palm, Chinese evergreen, English ivy, gerbera daisy, Janet Craig, mass cane, peace lily, pot mum, and mother-in-law's tongue. (NASA Clean Air Study, n.d.)

While the NASA study advised having fifteen to eighteen plants per 1800 square feet for maximum air scrubbing effectiveness, I think that's too many to be practical for most people. Just buy a few of your favorites and place them around. I name mine and talk to them. My Jim lost a leaf this week, and Susan spent more time in the corner. Studies have shown that singing to your houseplants can make them happier and grow better (I like Marvin Gaye). Note:

some plants are toxic to pets, so be careful and do your research!

For home renovations and building in general, it's important to be mindful of the toxic chemicals present in your choice of supplies. Many residential building products off-gas toxic chemicals long after they are installed, which is often called *sick building syndrome*. I always use a no-VOC paint from Benjamin Moore. For flooring, I personally like wood, slate, or tile, and then adding natural wool, jute, or sisal area rugs rather than nylon carpet. But if you already have carpet, don't worry about it—just be sure to vacuum it often. If you're installing flooring and then finishing it with something, make sure to use no- or low-VOC alternatives. Nowadays, they even make caulks that don't off-gas, so there's really no excuse for not being health conscious. These products are also better for the environment.

FINANCES

Webster's dictionary defines the word "abundance" as "an ample quantity; affluence or wealth; a relative degree of plentifulness." (Abundance, n.d.)

I think a lot about this word and how it relates to money. I think many of us, including myself, have a misunderstanding about money from our upbringing and society. Somehow, we know in our hearts that wealth can be connected to a better life, and in some cases a more spiritually enriched experience of philanthropy, but we don't understand why. Many wealthy people have been conditioned to feel guilty about how much they have. They may enjoy driving their nice car around town, but feel terrible when they pass a homeless person asking for money.

There is a famous Bible verse we have all heard from Timothy 6:10: "For the love of money is a root of all kinds of evil. Some people, eager for money, have wandered from the faith and pierced themselves with many griefs."

It's important to note that the verse says the *love* of money is the root of all evil, not money itself. Money is simply kinetic potential. *Greed* is the root of all evil because it causes people to hoard, deceive, and withhold wealth from those in need. This point has been clarified and popularized by wealth guru T. Harv Eker and teacher of *The Secret* Joe Vitale.

Since Ali Dede prescribed that I read T. Harv Eker's book *The Secrets of the Millionaire Mind*, I have believed that money is closer to the root of most good in the world. Most good things cost money. Eker points out that charities with no money rarely do anything at all.

Call me an optimist or idealist, but I think we're all meant to live abundant lives and that there would be more than enough to go around if the focus on attracting more wealth into our lives were made in conjunction with helping others. We need to come together for what's good and believe in the unbounded potential of the universe to carry us through. Now, I know people who aren't wealthy and yet live abundant lives because they know how to live well. I still feel they could expand on that. I know people in certain lines of work, especially governmental, often feel confined because they love their job but must accept a certain wage. Frankly, I think firemen and police should make fortunes for risking their lives every day. Until that day comes, I think we can all focus on alternative ways to create income in our spare time. If you're an trainer, you could make a webpage and YouTube channel that teaches people exercises and diet and write a book on it.

Abundance is our birthright, and we should strive to have all the luxuries we want in life. It may seem hard to do, but there's nothing bad about having a nice suit for yourself if you have the means. Yes, there are others in need in the world and we should help them with what we have, but it's also their duty to make changes in their lives to become wealthier *if they have the correct circumstances to do so*. All of us should alleviate the suffering of those in the direst circumstances around the world and lift them up so that they can then be in a position to have the best lives possible.

The Best Financial Blueprint

The best economic model according to Ali Dede is Robert Kiyosaki's, proven by his own success. Kiyosaki is the best-selling author of *Rich Dad Poor Dad* and many subsequent financial blockbusters. His economic model came from his childhood observations of his "rich dad" (a wealthy friend's father) and "poor dad" (his biological father). When he got into the real world, he followed the advice of his rich dad and studied the lives of other wealthy people. He found that rich people tend to invest their money in assets that generated cash flow, whereas poor and middle-class people tend to buy liability by overspending. He also found poor, middle, and even upper middle-class people tend to save money instead of wisely investing due to risk aversion and a fear of making mistakes. People with a "wealthy mind" will take extra money and invest it in a small business, oil drill, warehouse, foreclosed rental house, or trading in the market like a shark (buy low, sell high). For instance, Bill Bartmann is a billionaire who made his fortune in debt collection, went bankrupt, and made all his money back because he had a wealthy mind.

For Kiyosaki, a rich person is not someone who has money in the bank but a person who has money coming to them through passive investment income. Such people have more immunity to recessions or potential dollar crises, and at a certain level, will never have to work again.

Cash flow assets would include rental properties,

commodities like oil, royalties from personal property, profitable businesses like franchises, personal businesses, internet marketing, and stocks that pay dividends. Precious metals also tend to steadily rise while remaining immune to inflation and falling fiat currency.

Precious Metals

Since the 2008 economic recession, precious metals have gone through a boom. As faith in the US dollar—the reserve fiat currency for much of the world—declines, foreign countries have started investing in gold as a protection against inflation. Meanwhile, the printers at the US Federal Reserve keep printing paper money that isn't backed by anything, all the while borrowing money from China and Japan, who own a percentage of our debt and may push for a universal currency. The news drones on about how gold and silver aren't practical because they have no intrinsic value, yet people and countries always reach for them in times of economic uncertainty. Nixon pulled the plug on gold in 1971, and ever since, the dollar hasn't been tied to even an ounce of gold but rather to the printing press of the Federal Treasury.

I do feel that US currency will continue to steadily decline if the country's deficit isn't greatly reduced. Diversifying your assets into a certain percentage of gold and silver —say 10 percent minimum—will give you a hedge. I personally believe in owning more than that, but that's just me. This can take many forms: gold and silver coins, numismatic antique coins or bullion. Be careful when buying, though: many dealers will try to overcharge you on the market price. I have personally worked with Austin Gold Coins in Austin, Texas. You can also invest in gold ETFs like

GLD—an exchange-traded fund that holds gold and allows for trading on the stock market. You can also buy options this way, if you know how. But never only substitute an ETF or any other intangible market asset for actual metal in your possession somewhere close to you. Also, do some research in gold mining company stocks. This could be very useful in the future.

Jimmy Buffett's Empire

I want to recommend studying musician and businessman Jimmy Buffett's economic model because he follows Kiyosaki's financial model either consciously or unconsciously, and I feel it is beneficial to look at an example of someone well known who has successfully applied it. Almost no one knows that Buffett was a practically broke and struggling musician after his most famous hit, "Margaritaville." After being scalped by the record companies and blowing all his money on toys, he was sitting in his room one day trying to figure out what he could do next. He decided to write a book. That first book, *Tales from Margaritaville* published in 1989, went on to became a *New York Times* bestseller. Instead of investing his new riches in stocks and bonds like everyone else or spending them on toys, he got Kiyosaki wise and started investing in businesses. He opened the restaurant Margaritaville and it became very successful; he wrote more books (intellectual property)—all bestsellers; he started his own record company so he basically worked for himself; he started his own T-shirt, beer, and product line and sold them at his restaurants and concerts. (Buffett, 2000) And now, he's one of the most financially successful musicians in the world. *The Chicago Tribune* estimates he makes $40 million a year. Now that is how it's done.

13

TITHING

My grandfather's father, Robert D. Pearson, was a Baptist preacher in Mississippi who devoted his life to being of service both in and out of the church. When he wasn't in church, he was at the side of the sick and dying, holding their hands. Growing up, I spent a lot of time with his son, my grandfather Wilbur Pearson, who was always quoting Biblical scripture. My grandfather was no "Sunday Christian." When I was at his home, we prayed for people in need around the world, in the morning and the evening, every day, for long periods of time. Although my grandfather sometimes had a rigid view of spirituality in general, I always considered him to be spiritually oriented; he believed in the truth of his faith. He gave to those in need even though he wasn't a wealthy man himself. As a result, good things seemed to happen to him. True, sometimes people would take advantage of his generosity. I remember one time he sold a fishing boat to a man who told him he would pay for it later, but he never did. Such was his nature—my grandfather just let it go. He lived to be ninety-seven years old and avoided any major illnesses for the most part. His funeral was large and attended by many who praised his kindness.

I believe my grandfather's charity enriched his life. There is a verse about giving, Luke 6:38, which I am sure he knew: "Give, and it will be given to you. A good measure, pressed down, shaken together and running over, will be poured into your lap. For with the measure you use, it will be measured to you."

I believe that tithing returns to the giver because energy ebbs and flows. Positive energy creates a return of positive energy, and negative energy produces more of the same. Like will attract like. Money is energy too, which has a corresponding effect when it's spent.

Two of my financial mentors, Robert Kiyosaki and Joe Vitale, both recommend giving money as the best way to receive more of your own. Robert says that when he was down and out, he would write a check to a children's charity and within the next week, a financial windfall would come through. This is similar to the movie *Pay it Forward* (2000), where a teacher gives his class an assignment to try to change the world. One student comes up with the idea to "pay it forward" and the results are profound, effecting the whole nation.

T. Harv Eker suggests tithing 10 percent a month of your income to the charity or charities of one's choice, and I think that's a good model. If you can't give money, then give your time: volunteer.

Poor people often believe that wealthy people are greedy. While a culture of greed has been allowed to flourish in the United States and throughout the world, I think some rich people like Microsoft founder Bill Gates are among the most generous people in the world. Many spend their time making donations and setting up institutions for the disadvantaged and needy. Bill Gates, for his part, has pledged to give away most of his wealth during his lifetime.

I think my grandfather would have agreed that the important thing to remember when giving is that it's our duty as human beings to be of service to others. If not to learn and grow, then service is the real reason we're here. Altruism isn't just a spiritual act; we should pick up our fellow man because it's our humanity—he's us and we're him. One day, when we're in need of help, will we have made deposits in our spiritual bank account to withdraw from? There's a quote that Dede loves, from the African American scientist George Washington Carver: "How far you go in life depends on your being tender with the young, compassionate with the aged, sympathetic with the striving, and tolerant of the weak and strong. Because someday in your life you will have been all of these."

14

DATING, RELATIONSHIPS AND THE
BEST SEX

Theories on dating abound. With the popularity of online dating, there is no excuse to say you can't find a date anymore. I like online dating myself and know many people who have met their soul mates online. I personally met my wife, Wiphawan (her name means "radiance" in Thai), online, and we have the most wonderful connection. We are so deeply in love and happily married. Online dating changed my life in the best way possible. I am not suggesting that you will find the love of your life on one round of Tinder. A good friend of mine did marry a Tinder date and she is a truly good and wonderful lady. People seem to assume Tinder is for quick dating and hookups, and that may be true, but people tend to get what they assume. Nevertheless, you might want to invest in a Match.com account where people have to invest money to have an account with more personal information. The thing I despise about Tinder is that it almost solely based on physical appearances with the user swiping right or left from a quick photo. This is very shallow. Growing up in an appearance-based culture had such a profound effect on my life, I wrote a humorous fiction novel about it titled *Big John and the Fortune Teller*. Check it out on Amazon, you'll love it!

If you are looking for a strategy to get to know people and possibly have dates or even just healthier sex, I personally think the best strategy is to be friends with people, while flirting at the same time, even if you meet them on a dating site. This will keep you out of the dreaded "friend zone." When it comes to going out, I am a little old fashioned and think men should be gentleman: lead, hold open doors, pick up the check, be polite and courteous, etc. Men - be creative when taking women out. Think of fun activities like dancing, walking on the beach, hiking, or playing a game—things you can do together instead of just going to an expensive boring dinner and watching a movie. Focus on creative, interactive activities. We all love movies, but let's be honest: you aren't connecting with your date during the movie unless you have already established a close connection beforehand. I think most women are totally bored senseless from the line "Let's watch Netflix and chill."

The United States has an appearance-driven culture, and appearances are shallow. Growing up, I was ridiculed for having freckles and red hair. In the deep South, it seemed like everyone wanted to date a guy with a great tan and brown hair. Of course, such standards are always based on the prevailing cultural conditioning. If I had been in Ireland, I would have been a hot ticket! Always look beyond a person's outward form to their spiritual essence. Some of the most beautiful people in the world are some of the most boring, basic people you will ever met.

Furthermore, if you are romantically pursuing someone who isn't interested in you, you may be suffering from low self-esteem. One day back in 2006, my good friend Brad Yates reminded me just how many fish there are in the sea when I was complaining about a girl that didn't work out—there are literally billions of people in the world. If someone doesn't want you, then why would you still like them? Always take care of yourself first, and find someone who values you for who you are.

I believe the best book ever written on relationships is John Gray's *Men Are from Mars, Women Are from Venus*. John Gray states that men and women are hard-wired differently and so they want different things or prioritize differently. Women are more emotional beings and men more mental beings. This book is a must-read for anyone who has had trouble in a relationship, or even for someone who is in a wonderful relationship and just wants to make it better.

What it really comes down to is communication. Couples who communicate fall deeper in love, form stronger bonds, and resolve conflicts easily before they boil over into serious outbursts. If you've read John Gray's books and you're still having relationship troubles, many problems can be fixed with couples' counseling.

However, let's be clear that many people who break up for very good reasons get back together again just out of convenience, but they truly don't belong together. Sometimes, there are so many memories you share of happy times together that after separating, you review those memories instead of all the problems that ended the relationship. I say: move on. In his illustrious book *Advice from a Sufi*, Dede compares a bad relationship to mismatched animals. You may be a cat in a relationship with a hippopotamus, or a fox with a tiger. You need to be with someone who is on the same wavelength as you. If you have just broken up with someone, I suggest using the basic EFT recipe outlined in the beginning of this book and tapping as much as possible for all the emotions arising from the bad relationship until you are clear. Then, revaluate where you are. You may be able to try dating someone new for a change, or find yourself able to approach the old relationship in a new way.

Some people have truly bad vibrations and need to be moved away from. I asked Dede if I should reconnect with an old flame and he said, "Stay away from her. She is very far from being and being close to you."

Positive relationships often depend on one's horoscope (the time and birth of a person). You may want to look into this, as it can lead to harmonious relationships. There are exceptions to every rule, and some people whose horoscopes don't match up can still work out in real life. I have never even glanced at the horoscope for my wife and me—I just know we work.

Sex can be the most rewarding and satisfying experience in life, especially when there is a deep love and connection involved. However, despite being a perfectly natural desire that we should never be afraid of, it is also responsible for many problems in relationships and friendships.

Unfortunately, many men's sexual education and programming today comes from hardcore pornography, which is gross and often aggressive. I saw my first pornographic magazine at the age of ten or so—too early, at any rate. After feeling empty and lonely after many months of binge-watching porn, I pretty much stopped for good around 2005 (although I have relapsed some). Looking at porn can destroy people's lives, like it almost did mine. It's sad that these awful movies are our new reality about sex. For one, some men isolate themselves with their porn when they might be out on a date if they were living in 1930.

Some women and men alike have been sexually assaulted or raped as children or when they were older.

Such violence may lead to a person viewing sex as bad. Tapping with EFT can help to dissolve these perturbations. EFT is a wonderful tool for PTSD, and talk therapy can also help a person to become more natural with sex.

In the Taoist branch of The Great Tradition, Dede taught me that the concept behind *real tantra* is that the loss of semen gradually weakens a man over time. This often results in low sexual drive too early in life and erectile dysfunction. Real tantra, taught by experts like the Thai master Mantak Chia, teaches a man to have orgasms without ejaculating, as well as how to have multiple orgasms and full-body orgasms. This involves contracting one's PC muscles (pubococcygael muscles) while circulating energy around the micro-orbit (an energy channel in the body). Mantak Chia has a wonderful book about men's sexuality called *The Multi-Orgasmic Man*. In that book's counterpart, *The Multi-Orgasmic Woman*, he also teaches women how to control their orgasms and circulate their energy, resulting in better, more rewarding sex. Chia shows how a couple can exchange this sexual energy during lovemaking as well by circulating it around their and their partner's energy channels. In the Tantric tradition, Chia also has books with many sexual positions in them, and he goes deeply into foreplay as well.

If you are a male who has lost the drive to have sex, many times it's due to a lack of regular sex. Other times, it is hormonal. I am by no means an expert on hormones, but Suzanne Somers is. Look into some books by her if you feel this is an issue for you. Many people (both men and women) have claimed that taking hormone replacements can correct sexual dysfunction and have anti-aging effects as well. I suffered with erectile dysfunction terribly on and off for years. During that time, I was diagnosed with low testosterone (low T) and was prescribed a bio-identical form of testosterone. Unfortunately, it didn't resolve the ED. I also tried a human growth hormone (HGH) supplement and Cialis with no benefit. I eventually cured it by tapping a few times for four days in a row to a Brad Yates YouTube video titled "Sex Issues."

I also suggest carefully experimenting with daily ginseng, which can be a powerful erectile stimulant. For ED, men can also take products like Cialis, which is superior to Viagra in my opinion because Viagra works right after you take it whereas Cialis works for a whole twenty-four-hour period. Please talk with your doctor before starting any sort of health regimen or new medicine.

TRAVELING & THE WONDERFUL WORLD OF NATURE

Writer Tahir Shah periodically quotes a Moroccan proverb that I like: "Much travel is needed before the raw man is ripened." This sums up my feelings about the importance of travel. Born in Mississippi in 1980, I began traveling as an infant. My parents, Ken and Charme, who were both artists and creatives, wanted to show me the world and have me experience other cultures, and I am so grateful to them for giving me this.

When I was thirteen, we traveled all over Italy—to Milan, Rome, Florence, and Naples. My mom's brother, Wilbur Pearson Jr., lived in Florence in Tuscany at the time, and we visited him there. Italy had a profound impact on my childhood. The culture was so otherworldly compared to my life back home. The food was real and tasted so incredible. Most Italian eateries hand-make their bread and pasta almost daily with only four ingredients. This baked dough was unlike anything I had ever experienced. The most memorable moment of the trip was eating at Harry's Bar in Venice where I ordered carpaccio (thinly sliced raw meat with a light drizzle of fresh olive oil). I think the meal was $300 (not adjusted for inflation)!

I spent my childhood going to visit relatives in northern California and southeast Florida. As I got older, I continued to travel in an almost obsessive way. Different places had different energies, and I wanted to experience them all. When I first met Dede at 24 years of age, he asked me if there was any place near where I was living at the time where I felt very well, or if there was a church I could go to that had similar spiritual energy for health and well-being. I replied no, but that I had felt very well in Italy. He then advised I move to St. Augustine, Florida, (the oldest city in America) because a cosmic energy had been buried there centuries ago and there was energy there coming from the ocean. He stated at the time, "Negative people, places and things have to be moved away from." When I arrived, it felt like a place touched by heaven. I could feel God in the cracks of the sidewalks as I walked along the old cobblestone streets. Inner work was so easy there.

I lived in St. Augustine for some time and would eventually travel the US searching for other energetic areas. I found this energy to be most pronounced in Big Sur, Bel Air, and Beverly Hills, California. Since then, energies have shifted all over the world and you won't find that same energy in those places, although they are still wonderful places with very great vibes.

There are also places in the world that have a negative energy. The world is a place of duality: good and bad, heaven and hell, light and dark, positive and negative. The Sufi master Idries Shah said you can't truly know a place unless you close your eyes and stop your nose and ears up and silence yourself. I have been to a few places in the United States that have made me feel so uneasy. Some of them are full of wealth and abundance, so the eye can be a great trickster. I recommend always avoiding such places.

Travel as much as you like to experience the different energies and cultures all over the world. It will ripen you over time.

I believe that getting out into nature is one of the most important things for our well-being. Especially if you live in the city, you may need to get out to the country occasionally to reconnect and ground yourself, or at least visit city parks. Seeing wildlife, fishing, hunting, hiking, and gardening are all beneficial to the human spirit. I have framed photos taken in various places I have traveled of beautiful scenes from nature hanging on my walls because nature has such a positive frequency. Looking at them makes me feel elated.

Getting a minimum of fifteen minutes of daily sunshine is very good for the body. I personally find I need closer to an hour myself. The human body needs the "fire element," or the heat of the sun, to maintain wellness. If you live in Seattle or somewhere overcast, invest in a near-infrared light and use it every day to supplement the sun you're missing.

I own a 2018 Grand Design Reflection travel trailer that I take all over the USA on vacations to experience nature. When I am camping, I spend lots of time outside, cooking over an open flame. Camping is a wonderful way to get back in touch with nature and enjoy the outdoors. If you don't have the means to maintain a camper, don't worry—just pack a tent and sleeping bag and enjoy the campgrounds. You can hike around or explore the outdoors when you get there.

The Boy Scouts of America is a very special organization. Idries Shah actually lived in Robert-Baden Powell's house in the countryside of Kent, England. The house was a regular gathering place for many of Shah's well-known students such as Nobel Prize winning author Doris Lessing (1919 – 2003), *Catcher in the Rye* author JD Salinger (1919 – 2010) and a host of other characters. Unfortunately, the Boy Scouts organization has experienced some controversy concerning abuse allegations, which breaks my heart and makes me so sad. The Boys Scouts in my experience were always a good group for getting young people out into nature and teaching them "to do." As Dede says in his book *Advice from a Sufi*, learning "to do" is the most important thing a person can know. If one can do one thing well, one can do many other things.

16

YOUR OPTIMAL PLACE TO LIVE

I f you are already happy in the place where you live, then this chapter doesn't apply to you. But if you are looking to move in the future or are thinking about relocating, ask yourself, what do you want out of your place? Do you want to live near the ocean, the mountains, or the city? Maybe you love your hometown and want to live there. Maybe you're like the many people who are bound to a certain place by their jobs and thus limited in your options.

If you have the luxury of being able to live anywhere in the world, choose a place with good air quality first and foremost, in a country you deeply resonate with. Life is too short to breathe bad air in a place you don't like. Air is one of the five elements Ali Dede outlines for health. Within cities, this may mean paying more attention to certain neighborhoods. Traffic, walkability, bike trails, access to parks and nature, and amenities are all other things to carefully consider.

In my opinion, in America, California popularized the concept of lifestyle early on: middle aged fit men with sun bleached hair who lived and worked near the beach, surfed at daybreak, juiced carrots before work, walked or cycled to the office and would be off by noon to an around the corner salad shop in a cool but sunny 72 degrees. It makes sense then that the rugged, eco minded outdoor company Patagonia was founded in Santa Monica, California. The founder Yvon Chouinard has adopted this good lifestyle concept for himself and his employees, which he popularized in his business biography, *Let My People Go Surfing*. The book is titled after his motto that his employees in Ventura, California should be allowed to take surf breaks and wear no shoes around the office.

When renting an apartment, always choose a place that's not noisy but does have a good landlord who fixes things. Otherwise, renting can be hell. If buying, ask yourself, do you want a maintenance-free place like a condo or a wide-open grounds on some land outside the city? The bottom line is to get in touch with what you want and love and go for that. People are not the same. People want different things.

Always choose a building that is white or light colored. When I was very ill, Dede advised I wear only white clothing all the time and live in a white building with white walls. "Be known as The Man Who Wears White," he said. Colors follow the law of attraction. Light colors attract positive frequencies and darker colors attract darker energies. Race is completely obsolete in this equation. All human races are equal—our essences are the same.

17

DO WHAT YOU LOVE, LOVE WHAT YOU DO

A primary education, to a point, is very important for everyone. For those who live in an area where the public schools are dangerous, homeschooling in America may be a better option these days. A collegiate education is important if you want or need to learn certain professional skills or certifications to practice the profession you are pursuing. Certain ventures, however, such as opening a business or being an artist, do not necessarily require a collegiate education. Many of the most successful businesspeople left college early in order to pursue their dreams. I believe college is very important and its value should never be dismissed, but the individual should carefully consider what they want to do and make sure they are on the right track to pursue it, whether that means staying in school or not. I took a Photoshop course at the University of New Orleans that has helped me tremendously in performing graphic design for websites and product packaging. Without that class, I would be useless in design work. The important thing is to follow your heart and do what you love. Bliss will follow. It has been said, "If you do what you love, you will never work a day in your life."

It is also useful to do something professionally that serves others or society in some way. Do not be prideful about being of service, rather see it as a duty. I also think it's useful to leave a legacy behind for generations to come. These days, anyone can do this with YouTube and self-publishing. You can post a video on YouTube and it will be there for many years to come—maybe forever.

18

BEING OF SERVICE

W e spoke about the importance of tithing in the financial section. Now, what are some other ways we can help the world? As we go through our day, let's think of ways we might be able to effect positive change. Let's develop think tanks with friends for this. You could also volunteer your time or come up with projects. There are many nonprofits out there looking for ideas. Collaborate with them. I have found two very important concepts for helping the world that I want to share with you, which came from my teacher Ali Dede.

The first involves giving you an overview of the so-called "broken window theory" and Manhattan's crime problem in the 1980s before it became one of the safest cities to live in the US. Although, Mayor Michael Bloomberg initiated a stop and frisk policy that many consider to be racially biased in the 2000's, violent crime in the city had dropped by the end of the 90's.

George L. Kelling coauthored an article titled "Broken Windows" in the 1980s, which basically outlined that if a building has a few broken windows that aren't fixed in a timely manner, eventually vandals will break more windows. I went to boarding school in New England in Kent, Connecticut, and I remember going to New York City often in 1996 until I graduated in 1999, and it was still unsafe then. One time, after arriving at The Port Authority, I had a man approach me only to grab my suitcase and walk off with it. I ran after him, and when I caught up to him, he demanded money. Somehow, I managed to grab my suitcase from him and run inside a hotel lobby behind me. For a fifteen-year-old, the experience was quite unsettling.

In the 1990s, William Bratton became the head of NYC transit—Kelling was his mentor. He began implementing zero-tolerance policies in the grimy, run-down, crime infested, graffiti-splattered NYC subways. Things improved.

Mayor Giuliani got elected and hired Bill Bratton as his commissioner; together, they employed a zero-tolerance policy (arresting drunks and subway fare evaders, painting over graffiti) in the bad areas of the city. Things improved.

By 2000, crime rates in NYC had fallen and it was a safe place to live. Harlem blossomed into a new urban neighborhood of internet book cafes and organic co-ops. Bill Clinton opened an office there. (Broken Windows Theory, n.d.)

Ten years later, New York was one of the safest cities in the US.

"Cleanliness is next to Godliness." We've all heard that, but do we believe it? Why are crime-ridden areas always full of broken windows, graffiti, weeds, and litter, and safe areas are usually clean?

Does seeing broken windows create a broken mind? What happened in New York, and how can we use those lessons to stop crime in the most dangerous cities in the world?

I believe that if we implement clean-up campaigns in

the most dangerous cities across the world, those neighborhoods will improve. Spread the word about New York's broken windows.

The second project I am interested in involves hunger in Africa. In 2010, sub-Saharan Africa had 239 million hungry people. I think it's a real lesson in gratitude for Americans to just take five minutes to reflect on that—239 million people who didn't have enough food.

What's the cause? Drought has put a strain on agriculture, and wars and crooked politicians have dragged various countries to their knees.

What's the cure? Starving people need water and food, so you must address that problem or else people die. There's a very fine organization called Stop Hunger Now and another called WFP that deliver packaged food to starving people in Africa. The Gates Foundation is also hard at work to provide sanitizing toilets and drinkable water to people in need. You might choose one of these charities as the recipients of your tithing (I have not given to them, so I can't say).

But I think one of the most overlooked solutions for nutrition in Africa may be *Moringa oleifera,* or the Tree of Life. The seeds of this very interesting plant could be planted all over for its wide-ranging utility. Moringa is the most nutritionally dense food in the world. It can grow in the most arid conditions with very little water, which makes it perfect for Africa's desert regions. Scientists have confirmed that gram for gram, the powder from its leaves contain four times the calcium in milk, four times the vitamin A in carrots, seven times more vitamin C than oranges, two times the protein in milk, and three times the potassium in bananas—not to mention seven of the essential amino acids, trace minerals, and antioxidants. (Levy J. , Moringa Benefits Hormonal Balance, Digestion, Mood and

More, 2020) I have personally taken this nutrient a lot with great results—increased energy, stamina, and well-being. It is known in Africa as "Mother's Helper" because if a malnourished mother takes the powder, she can produce milk again and avoid a malnourished infant. What can you do? Spread the word about the Tree of Life.

19

RELAXATION & A SPIRITUAL PATH

In the modern world, sometimes it's hard to not get stressed out. How can we ease stress? We've already discussed EFT, Bach flower remedies, and HeartMath in previous chapters. Exercise or massage can be other good ways to get out of the mind and into the body also. A bath is a helpful way to relax the muscles, meditate, reflect on the day, slow down, and just plain get clean!

In my old house, I used to have candles of different sizes, shapes, and colors in every room. I would light them for a certain amount of time every night when I performed inner work because the glow produced is truly magnificent and calming. Candles made from beeswax are truly superior because they produce a better glow as well as negative ions and these are useful for inner work as well. I used to find unique vases from Pier 1, Pottery Barn, and Crate and Barrel that would splinter and ricochet the light to increase this effect. Be sure to extinguish them all before leaving the room or going to sleep.

Finding a spiritual path in the year 2000 changed my life in innumerable ways, which I detail in the first book in this series. I suggest you search for the path that suits you. My path is the way of the Sufi, though I cannot call myself one —I am a student still. Much of the content from this book is derived from reading material suggested to me by my teacher Ali Dede. His form of pure Sufism goes back to the time of Adam and has had many different names throughout history. There are many diluted and even down-right phony schools of thought that would call themselves "Sufi" today, but the real stream of truth can still be found, such as that preserved by the ancestors of Jan Fishan Khan.

The important thing is for you to find the way to God that speaks to you, whether it be Buddhist or Sufi or even a personal path of growth and enlightenment. I personally believe having the assistance of a guide makes traveling the way much easier. Sometimes it is almost impossible to see yourself correctly from the outside. I find it quite baffling that people hire teachers and coaches for all manner of pursuits, but when it comes to inner work, they feel they don't need any help. Quite the opposite is usually true. In this area, it is even more useful and even necessary to have a guide.

You may enjoy working with some of Dede's exercises on his special YouTube channel, The Sufi Tradition—found under the Gifts section of my website, www. duketateauthor.com.

Another very beneficial spiritual exercise is *ho'ponopono*, the Hawaiian radical forgiveness technique made popular by the law of attraction teacher Joe Vitale in his amazing book *Zero Limits*. The idea behind ho'oponopono is that everything that shows up for you in the world, you have manifested; therefore, you can change it by making amends with the divine. This is done through a mantra to God that goes, "I love you, I am so sorry, please forgive me, thank you." This is repeated over and over again while focusing on the issue. After performing this technique for some time, I often experience the sensation of energy in my body and being. I believe profound clearings can occur as a result of this work.

Also sent to me by Dede, quantum entrainment, developed by Frank Kinslow, is a truly miraculous self-realization tool. By it, Frank teaches many methods to grow spiritually. I have used his techniques and exercises over the years and have read a number of his incredible books, always with truly wonderful results. I suggest you familiarize yourself with his work and try his recommendations for yourself. You won't be disappointed.

20

CONCLUSION

I hope at least some of the material in this book that I learned over many years from my Sufi teacher Dede has been able to help you in some way. Dede is a brilliant diagnostician and very knowledgeable about health, diet, nutrients, and life in general. Every day I spoke to him, I learned something new and useful. His versatility surprises me in a good way.

Life is about choices. Make the right choices, with intention, and you will get wonderful results. Life is also full of mystery, happy accidents, and synchronicities—and unfortunately, unpredictable tragedies. Try to remember that life may not always be in your control, even when you are using the law of attraction and your intentions. There is an Eastern saying: "Trust in God, but tie your camel first." I think that is a wonderful motto for how to approach the world. Always be careful in life, intend and want the best for you and your companions, your loved ones, and your country, make wise choices, and you will get the best results possible. Be careful, but don't be boring or inflexible. Smile and have fun! Life is good, as the saying goes—but as my guide says, only if we *make it so.*

RECOMMENDED READING

Alt, Carol. *Eating in the Raw: A Beginner's Guide to Getting Slimmer, Feeling Healthier, and Looking Younger the Raw-Food Way*. New York: Clarkson Potter, 2004.

Barron, Jon. *Lessons from the Miracle Doctors*. Laguna Beach, CA: Basic Health Publications, 2008.

Callahan, Roger. *Thought Field Therapy*. McGraw Hill, 2001.

Campbell, T. Colin, and Thomas M. Campbell II. *The China Study: The Most Comprehensive Study of Nutrition Ever Conducted and the Startling Implications for Diet, Weight Loss, and Long-Term Health*. Dallas, TX: BenBella Books, 2006.

Dede, Ali. *Advice from a Sufi*. www.thesufitradition.com. Available in English, Russian, and Spanish editions.

Diamandis, Peter, and Steven Kotler. *Abundance: The Future Is Better Than You Think*. New York: Free Press, 2012.

Eker, T. Harv. *Secrets of the Millionaire Mind: Mastering the Inner Game of Wealth.* New York: HarperCollins, 2005.

Gallo, Fred, and Harry Vincenzi. *Energy Tapping.* Oakland, CA: New Harbinger Publications, 2000.

Gray, John. *Men Are from Mars, Women Are from Venus.* New York: HarperBusiness, 1995.

Kinslow, Frank. *The Kinslow System: Your Path to Proven Success in Health, Love, and Life.* Carlsbad, CA: Hay House, 2013.

Kiyosaki, Robert. *Rich Dad's Conspiracy of the Rich: The 8 New Rules of Money.* Scottsdale, AZ: Plata Publishing, 2009.

Kiyosaki, Robert. *Rich Dad, Poor Dad: What the Rich Teach Their Kids about Money that the Poor and Middle Class Do Not!* New York: Warner Books, 1997.

Lin, Chunyi. *Spring Forest Qi-Gong, Level 1: For Health.* Minnetonka, MN: Learning Strategies Corporation, 2000.

Palmer, Helen. *Enneagram: Understanding Yourself and the Others in Your Life.* New York: HarperCollins, 1988.

Pratt, Stephen, and Kathy Matthews. *SuperFoods Rx: Fourteen Foods That Will Change Your Life.* New York: HarperCollins, 2004.

Sears, Barry, and Bill Lawren. *Enter the Zone: A Dietary Road Map.* New York: HarperCollins, 1995.

Shah, Idries. *The Exploits of the Incomparable Mulla Nasrudin.* London: ISF Publishing, 1966.

Shah, Idries. *The Sufis.* London: ISF Publishing, 1964.

Shah, Idries. *World of Nasrudin.* London: ISF Publishing, 2003.

Shah, Tahir. *Jinn Hunter.* London: Secretum Mundi Publishing, 2019.

Shah, Tahir. *Scorpion Soup.* London: Secretum Mundi Publishing, 2013.

Shah, Tahir. *Travels with Nasrudin.* Bath, UK: Secretum Mundi Publishing, 2019.

Shimoff, Marci. *Happy for No Reason: 7 Steps to Being Happy from the Inside Out.* New York: Free Press, 2008.

Somers, Suzanne. *Ageless: The Naked Truth about Bioidentical Hormones.* New York: Crown Publishing Group, 2006.

Somers, Suzanne. *Bombshell: Explosive Medical Secrets that will Redefine Aging.* New York: Crown Publishing Group, 2012.

Vitale, Joe. *The Key: The Missing Secret for Attracting Anything You Want.* Hoboken, NJ: John Wiley & Sons, 2008.

RESOURCES

Clickable links to all resources included in this book can be found at: https://www.duketateauthor.com/gifts

Idries Shah Foundation

Teaching stories and Sufi books by Idries Shah are available through the nonprofit Idries Shah Foundation (ISF) on their website at
https://idriesshahfoundation.org/

Hoopoe Books

I also consider Hoopoe Books, an outreach of the Institute for the Study of Human Knowledge (ISHK), to be one of the best charities in the world today. Since 2007, this organization has distributed over 4.7 million children's books of a spiritual nature to children in Afghanistan. Education and reading changes young people's lives, and these youth are the future of the world. Donate to them, please.

Ali Dede

Ali Dede's website is
www.sufismo.com

WORKS CITED

Abundance. (n.d.). Retrieved from Merrian-Webster: https://www.merriam-webster.com/dictionary/abundance

Anxiety Association of America. (n.d.). Retrieved from www.adaa.org: https://adaa.org/living-with-anxiety/managing-anxiety

Axe, D. (2019, March 22). *Top 11 Omega 3 Benefits and How to Get More Omega 3 in Your Diet*. Retrieved from www.draxe.com: https://draxe.com/nutrition/supplements/omega-3-benefits-plus-top-10-omega-3-foods-list/

Axe, D. J. (2017, March 17). *Resveratrol: The Anti-Aging Power-house that's Good for the Heart, Brain and Waistline*. Retrieved from Dr. Axe: https://draxe.com/nutrition/all-about-resveratrol/

Barron, J. (n.d.). *Clinical Studies Reveal First, Natural Formula Effective for Removing Heavy Metals*. Retrieved from Baseline of Health Foundation: https://www.jonbarron.org/clinical-

study-reveals-first-natural-formula-proven-effective-
removing-hazardous-heavy-metals-new

Broken Windows Theory. (n.d.). Retrieved from Wikipedia:
https://en.wikipedia.org/wiki/Broken_windows_theory

Buffett, J. (2000). *A Pirate Looks At Fifty*. Ballantine Books.

Cafasso, J. (n.d.). *Mouthbreathing: Sympptoms, Complications
and Treatments*. Retrieved from Healthline: https://www.
healthline.com/health/mouth-breathing

*Clinical Study Reveals First, Natural Formula Effective For
Removing Heavy Metals*. (2005, October 25). Retrieved from
Baseline of Health Foundation: https://www.jonbarron.org/
clinical-study-reveals-first-natural-formula-proven-effective-
removing-hazardous-heavy-metals-new

Cousens, D. G. (n.d.). *The Universal and Holistic Super
Mineral*. Retrieved from Gabriel Cousens, MD: wwww.tree-
oflifecenterus.com

*Everett Storey: Turning the Harmful into Something that Saves
Lives*. (2016, July 15). Retrieved from Everett Storey.

Fife, B. (2013). *The Coconut Oil Miracle*. New York: Avery.

Flanagan, D. G. (2016). *Elixir of the Ageless: You Are What You
Drink*. Create Space.

Griffin, G. E. (1974). *World Without Cancer; The Story of B17*.
American Media.

Intrepretive Summary – Listeria Monocytogenes Risk Assessment. (2003). *Center for Food Safety and Applied Nutrition*, 17.

Levy, J. (2019, May 15). *Magnesium Benefits, Dosage, Recommendation and Best Types*. Retrieved from www.draxe.com: https://draxe.com/nutrition/magnesium-supplements/

Levy, J. (2019, June 3). *What Is CoQ10? 8 Benefits for Energy, Aging, and Brain and Heart Health*. Retrieved from Dr. Axe: https://draxe.com/nutrition/all-about-coq10/

Levy, J. (2020, February 21). *Moringa Benefits Hormonal Balance, Digestion, Mood and More*. Retrieved from Dr. Axe: https://draxe.com/nutrition/moringa-benefits/

Link, R. (2018, April 16). *Vitamin C Benefits the Immunse System and So Much More*. Retrieved from Dr. Axe: https://draxe.com/nutrition/vitamin-c-benefits/

NASA Clean Air Study. (n.d.). Retrieved from Wikipedia: https://en.wikipedia.org/wiki/NASA_Clean_Air_Study

Ruggeri, C. (2019, September 17). *Cayene Pepper Benefits Your Gut, Heart and More*. Retrieved from www.draxe.com: https://draxe.com/nutrition/herbs/cayenne-pepper-benefits/

Schmid, R. (2009). *The Untold Story of Raw Milk: The History, Politics and Science of Nature's Perfect Food*. New Trends Publishing.

Steven G. Pratt, M. (2006). *SuperFoods RX: Fourteen Foods That Will Change Your Life*. New York: Harper.

The Device and the Inventor. (n.d.). Retrieved from www.the-quantumpulse.com: https://www.
thequantumpulse.com/about.html

Understand the Facts. (n.d.). Retrieved from Anxiety and
Depression Association of America: https://adaa.org/
understanding-anxiety

ABOUT THE AUTHOR

Duke Tate was born in Mississippi where he grew up surrounded by an age-old tradition of storytelling common to the deep South. He currently lives in Southeast Florida where he enjoys fishing, surfing, cooking Asian food and reading.

You can view his YouTube channel here and his author website here.

a amazon.com/Duke-Tate

g goodreads.com/9784192.Duke_Tate

f facebook.com/duketateauthor

twitter.com/duke_tate

ALSO BY DUKE TATE

Big John and the Fortune Teller

The Opaque Stones

Returning to Freedom: Breaking the Bonds of Chemical Sensitivities and Lyme Disease

The Alchemy of Architecture: Memories and Insights from Ken Tate

Coming Soon:

Ken Tate in Black and White

Life Lessons from a Blue Macaw: Learning to Live in the Now